Contents

Whales

Whales are close relatives of dolphins and porpoises. There are many types of whale in the world's oceans.

Whales have flippers, a long body and no back limbs.

Blue whale

The blue whale grows up to 30 metres long and weighs as much as 160 tonnes – that's the same as 20 African elephants.

Marine mammals

Whales are **mammals**. They are unusual mammals as they live in water, but still breathe air. All mammals have at least some hairs on their bodies. Whales have just a few bristles in their nostrils.

A baby whale is called a calf.

This baby beluga whale is about to drink milk from its mother.

Breaching

Whales often leap out of the water. This is called **breaching**.

Types of whale

There are about 50 different **species**, or kinds, of whales. They are divided into two groups – toothed whales and baleen whales.

Toothed whales, such as this orca, have small teeth used for gripping fish and other prey.

FANTASTIC FACT

Sperm whales prey on giant squid. The squid can be up to 18 metres long, and they fight with the whales. Scars from their suckers have been found on the skin of sperm whales.

Baleen whales

Baleen whales include humpback whales, grey whales and fin whales. Instead of teeth, they have huge baleen plates, fringed with hairs, hanging from their jaws. The plates sieve food from the water.

Toothed whales

This group includes sperm whales, pilot whales, beluga whales, narwhals and orcas (killer whales). They are smaller than the baleen whales and do not have plates in their mouths. Toothed whales are **predators** that hunt fish, squid and seals.

Long tusk

The narwhal is an unusual toothed whale because it has a tusk. The tusk is actually a very long, straight tooth.

Where whales live

Whales are found in all the oceans of the world, including the coldest oceans, such as the Southern and Arctic Oceans.

Orcas prefer colder waters.

Cold water food

Cold water is rich in food for whales, such as krill and plankton. Krill are prawnlike creatures eaten by baleen whales. Plankton are tiny animals and plants that float in the water. Some whales eat plankton. Others eat the fish that feed on plankton.

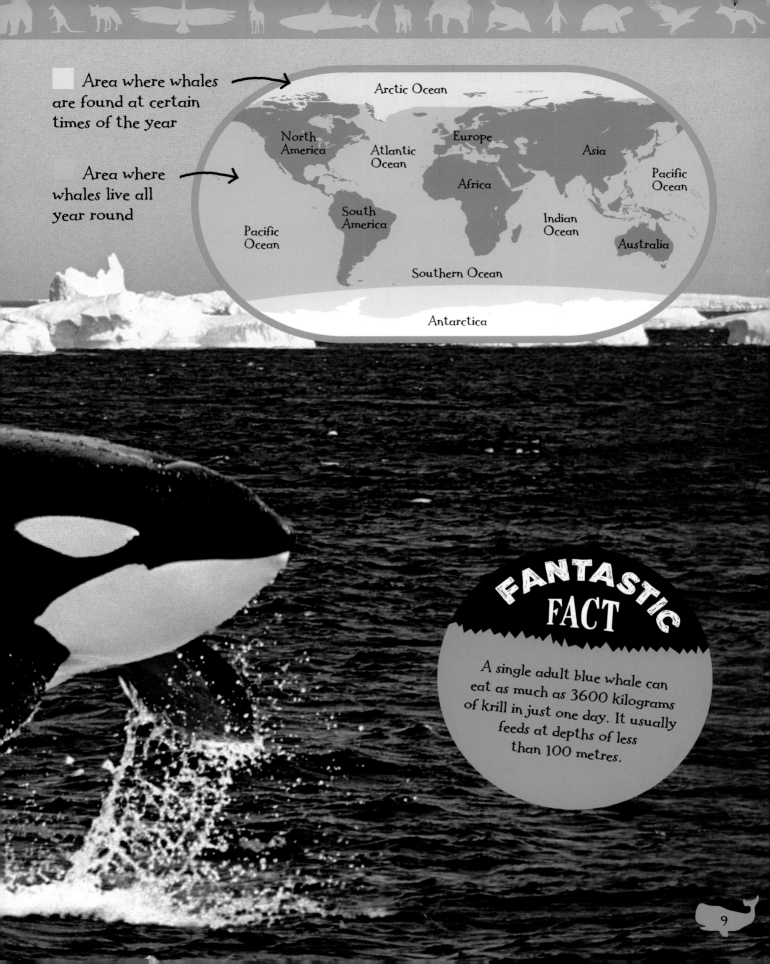

Area where whales are found at certain times of the year

Area where whales live all year round

Arctic Ocean

North America

Atlantic Ocean

Europe

Asia

Pacific Ocean

Africa

Pacific Ocean

South America

Indian Ocean

Australia

Southern Ocean

Antarctica

FANTASTIC FACT

A single adult blue whale can eat as much as 3600 kilograms of krill in just one day. It usually feeds at depths of less than 100 metres.

Giving birth

Female whales may be **pregnant** for between 9 and 17 months, depending on the species. As soon as her **calf** is born, the mother pushes it to the surface for its first breath of air.

A baby sperm whale is about 4 metres long when it is born.

FANTASTIC FACT

Female Californian grey whales give birth in the shallow waters off the coast of Mexico. The shallow water is thought to protect the calves from sharks.

Born headfirst

Many female whales swim to a special place where they give birth to a single calf. The calf is born headfirst.

Learning to swim

The calf stays close to its mother's side for the first month or so. It practises swimming and, after six weeks, it can do a complete roll underwater.

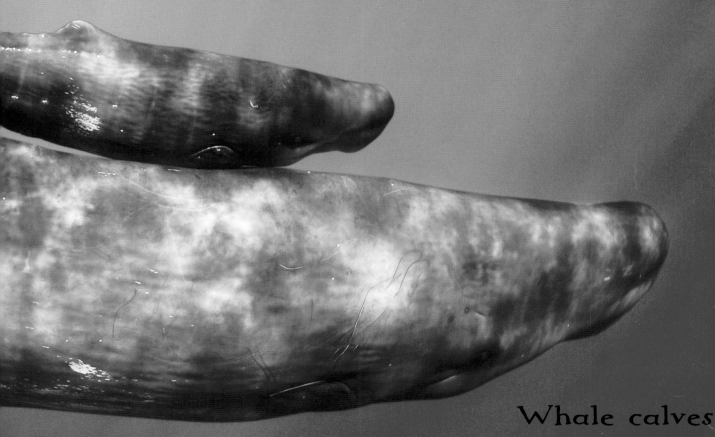

Whale calves

A mother whale feeds her calf on milk that is rich in fat, so it grows quickly. The calf has to learn how to breathe without swallowing water, and also how to stay upright in the water.

Growing up

Whale calves feed on their mother's milk for up to a year. Then they start to eat adult food. This is called **weaning**.

Orcas have been seen to jump as high as 4 metres into the air while hunting dolphins to eat.

Playful behaviour

Young right whales have been seen to breach (jump out of the water) more than 80 times an hour while playing.

Staying close

By staying close to their mother, whale calves learn where to find food and which routes to take on long journeys. Some calves leave their mother when they are weaned, but sperm whale calves stay close for 10 years.

Leaping and splashing

Young orca calves like this one are very playful. They love to jump out of the water and smash down with a loud splash. They roll in the water, too, and slap the surface with their fins.

13

Underwater living

Unlike fish and other underwater animals, whales cannot breathe in water. They must swim to the surface to breathe air. Whales do not breathe through their mouth, but through a large nostril called a **blowhole**.

Blowhole

A whale's blowhole is on the top of its head. Just before the whale dives underwater, a flap covers the blowhole.

Spurting water

Whales can stay underwater for a long time. When they come to the surface, they breathe out so hard that a jet of air and water bursts out of the blowhole.

Sperm whale

Spermaceti

Sperm whales have a huge, square head, filled with a waxy substance called spermaceti. This substance helps with **echolocation**, as it helps sound to travel.

Keeping warm

Whales have to keep warm in cold water. They have a thick layer of fat, called **blubber**, under their skin. The fat traps heat in the whale's body so the whale stays warm.

FANTASTIC FACT

Sperm whales can dive deeper than any other mammal in the world. Most dives are between 300 and 600 metres, but they can reach at least 2000 metres.

Swimming

Whales have a **streamlined** body shape that slips easily through the water. They have flippers rather than front legs, which they use to steer as they swim.

How whales swim

A whale's tail is made up of two flat fins, called flukes. Powerful muscles in the whale's back move the flukes up and down, and this pushes the whale through the water.

A whale's tail has a notch where the two flukes come together. →

Speed

The fastest large whale is the fin whale. It can swim at 48 kilometres per hour in short bursts when it is frightened. Normally it swims at about 30 kilometres per hour – the speed that a car drives through a town.

The largest flukes are those of the blue whale. They are just under 8 metres wide.

FANTASTIC FACT

There are no bones in the tail flukes of a whale. The tail moves up and down, unlike a fish's tail, which moves left and right.

17

Senses

Whales have well-developed senses that help them to find out about their surroundings. Their hearing is especially sensitive.

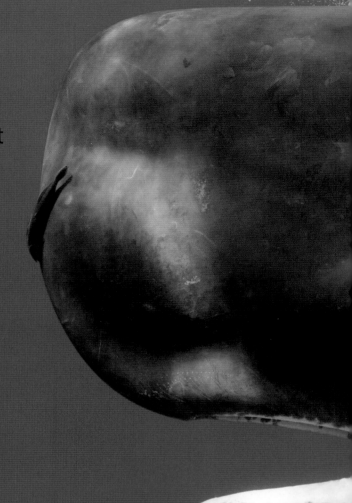

Echolocation

Toothed whales send out high-pitched clicks. These clicks bounce off objects and return to the whale as an echo. By listening to the echoes, the whale can work out the shape and position of objects, including prey.

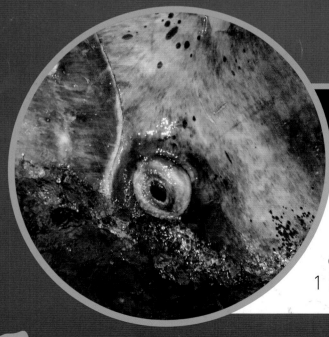

Eyes

Whales have small eyes and cannot see very well. This is not a problem, as they often swim in dark water, where they can see objects only up to about 1 metre away.

Ear hole

Ear holes

Whales do not have ears on the outside of their heads. Instead they have two tiny openings that lead to internal ears.

Submarines find their way around the oceans using a form of echolocation, called sonar.

19

Plankton feeders

Baleen whales eat plankton, krill and small fish. Hundreds of baleen plates form a curtain hanging from the whale's upper jaw. The whale swallows a huge mouthful of water and forces it through the plates, trapping the food contained in the water.

Krill

Krill are only 5 centimetres long, but they swim in vast swarms. These tiny creatures are preyed on by whales, fish, seals and penguins.

FANTASTIC FACT

The bowhead whale has the largest mouth of any animal. It's so big that a minibus could drive into it! This giant whale's baleen plates are 4.6 metres long.

Grey whale

The grey whale is the only bottom-feeding whale. It scoops up huge mouthfuls of mud from the seabed and sieves it to find food.

Working together

Humpback whales often work together to catch krill and fish. They blow bubbles to form a 'net' around their prey. Then the whales swim up through the centre of the bubble net and swallow the food in huge gulps.

This group of humpback whales has found a shoal of fish and is busy feeding.

Giant predators

Toothed whales are all predators. They hunt mainly for fish and squid. Their teeth are small and pointed – ideal for gripping slippery prey. These whales swallow their food whole or in large chunks.

An orca may eat as many as eight seal pups a day.

FANTASTIC FACT

Sperm whales often have scars on their sides caused by the suckers and beaks of struggling giant squid, one of their favourite foods.

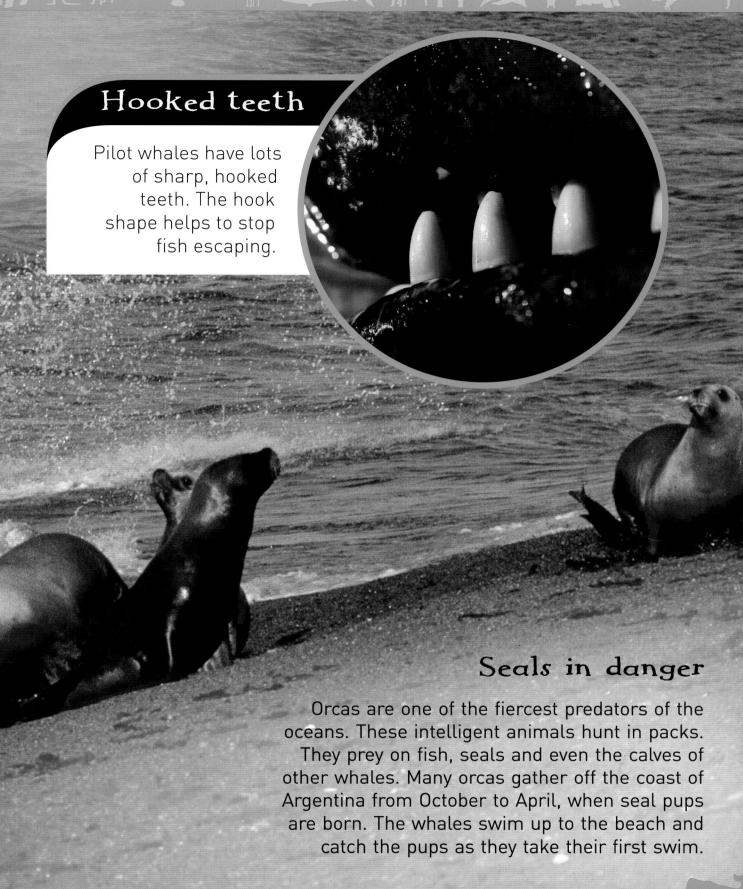

Hooked teeth

Pilot whales have lots of sharp, hooked teeth. The hook shape helps to stop fish escaping.

Seals in danger

Orcas are one of the fiercest predators of the oceans. These intelligent animals hunt in packs. They prey on fish, seals and even the calves of other whales. Many orcas gather off the coast of Argentina from October to April, when seal pups are born. The whales swim up to the beach and catch the pups as they take their first swim.

Communication

Whales communicate in many ways. They make different sounds, such as whistles, trills, moans and squeals. These sounds travel great distances through the water.

Humpback whales sing as they swim along.

Loudest animal

The moans of the blue whale register 180 decibels. This is the loudest sound made by any animal and is much louder than a jet engine.

Lobtailing

One way that whales communicate with each other is by lobtailing. The whale sticks its tail out of the water and then slaps it on the water's surface to make a loud sound.

FANTASTIC FACT

At certain depths, a whale's songs can travel for thousands of kilometres through the water. The sounds can cross whole oceans.

Humpback songs

Male humpback whales can sing! Their song contains up to 30 different sounds and it can last for 30 minutes. When the whale gets to the end of his song, he starts from the beginning again.

Whale journeys

Many whales spend part of the year feeding in cold water. Then they swim to warmer waters, where the females give birth to their calves. This journey is called a **migration**.

Spyhopping

From time to time, whales pop their head out of the water to check for landmarks and to see if there are other whales around. This is called spyhopping.

Return journey

After spending several months in warm water, the whales swim back to their feeding areas. They swim together in groups and follow the same routes each year.

Migration routes

Winter breeding grounds

FANTASTIC FACT

Grey whales migrate the farthest. They swim as much as 20,400 kilometres each year, from the Arctic to Mexico and back again.

Whales under threat

All around the world whales are under threat. For hundreds of years, they were hunted for their oil and meat. So many whales were killed that many species almost became **extinct**.

FANTASTIC FACT

The Californian grey whale is one of the few animals that has been taken off the list of **endangered** animals because its numbers have increased.

These people are watching grey whales off the coast of California.

www.kuyima.com

28

Trapped

Whales sometimes get caught in fishing nets or hurt by the propellers of ships. They also suffer when people take too much fish from the sea and do not leave enough for whales and other sea animals.

Conservation

In 1986, whaling was banned and whale numbers started to increase. Sadly, some countries want to start whaling again. It is important that whales are protected and whaling does not start again.

Life cycle of a whale

Whales have a long pregnancy, so they only give birth to a calf every two or three years. The calves stay with their mother for up to 10 years. They grow slowly and many are not ready to breed until they are 20 years old.

baby calf with mother

young calf

adult whale

Glossary

blowhole the nostril of a whale, on the top of its head

blubber a thick layer of fat under the skin

breaching when a whale jumps above the surface of the water

calf a baby or young whale

echolocation a way of finding where things are by sending out sounds and listening for echoes that come back

endangered in danger of dying out

extinct no longer any left alive

mammals animals that give birth to live young, rather than laying eggs; female mammals produce milk to feed their young

migration a journey that an animal makes each year to find food or to breed

predator an animal that hunts other animals for food

pregnant having a baby or babies developing inside

species one particular type of animal

streamlined having a long, narrow and smooth shape that slips easily through water

weaning changing from milk to an adult diet

Index